Inside the Synagogue

by Grace R. Freeman
and Joan G. Sugarman

Photography by Justin E. Kerr
and others

Illustrations by Judith Oren

Union of American Hebrew
Congregations • New York

Library of Congress Catalog Card Number 62-19996

Copyright 1963, by

THE UNION OF AMERICAN HEBREW CONGREGATIONS
New York, N.Y.

PRODUCED IN THE U.S. OF AMERICA

Seventh Printing, 1978

THIS BOOK

IS

DEDICATED

TO THE

CHILDREN

WE HAVE TAUGHT

AND

FROM WHOM WE

HAVE LEARNED SO MUCH.

—GRACE R. FREEMAN
—JOAN G. SUGARMAN

SECOND EDITION, 1965

The need to publish a second edition of INSIDE THE SYNAGOGUE so soon after its first appearance bespeaks the great value of this book and reflects great credit on its authors and its editors. Nonetheless, a number of editorial revisions had to be made and we wish to thank Rabbis Jack Bemporad, Erwin L. Herman and Mrs. Maurice Samuel for their many valuable suggestions.

—RABBI ALEXANDER M. SCHINDLER

PICTURE CREDITS: The obtaining of the photographs for *Inside the Synagogue* was only possible through the courtesy of many people. We especially want to thank Rabbi Lawrence W. Schwartz and Mr. Jacob W. Salz of the Jewish Community Center of White Plains, New York, where many of the pictures were taken.

We also are indebted to B'nai Israel Congregation of Bridgeport, Connecticut.

The cover and the bulk of the photographs were the work of Justin E. Kerr, with the exception of the following pictures which were gathered from other sources.

The Synagogue Architectural Library of the UAHC supplied the photographs for the following pages: Four, upper; eight; ten, upper left; ten, lower; eleven, lower; twelve, center; thirteen, lower; fifteen.

The Jewish Museum, Frank J. Darmstaedter, photographer: Seven, upper; fourteen; sixteen, upper; twenty; twenty five; twenty six; twenty seven.

Keeping Posted: Seven, lower; sixteen, lower.

Herbert S. Sonnenfeld, photographer: Thirteen, upper.

Keneseth Israel, Philadelphia, Pa.: Twenty three, lower left.

Congregation Sinai, Milwaukee, Wisc.: Twenty four.

EDITOR'S INTRODUCTION

The most immediate visible symbol of Judaism in the Western world is the synagogue. The ghetto having happily disappeared and the Jew having taken his place among the citizens of his country, little remains to distinguish the Jewish neighborhood or the Jewish individual from his surroundings.

The synagogue, too, has been transformed in this procession of acculturation. Its architecture is derivative of contemporary style and the proportion and arrangement of its rooms follow the American patterns of synagogue activity. Despite its altered structure, the synagogue retains its Jewish soul. The wealth of Jewish symbolism, the meanings, messages, and challenges which they disclose, the uses to which they invite us, all speak of that ancient way which joins each synagogue to Sinai.

The synagogue has always been this mixture of what seemed contemporary with what was known to be eternal. In our own day it has special significance in this regard because there are so few other reminders of Judaism's eternal task and, alas, so few other places where Jews join together in its accomplishment.

To help the young child appreciate what the synagogue is and has been, what it means and what it evokes, is the purpose of this beautiful and informed volume.

RABBI EUGENE B. BOROWITZ,
Director of Education

One

God's House Is Called a Synagogue

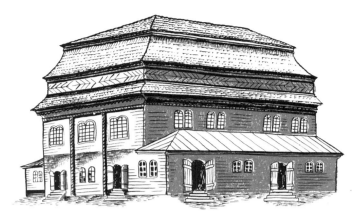

Ancient Wooden Synagogue in Poland

God is everywhere. He is in our homes and our schools, in the city and in the country.

We may pray to God anywhere. But there is a special house where Jewish boys and girls can go to pray to Him —a House of God. Sometimes it is called a **synagogue.** Sometimes it is called a **temple.** But both names mean the same—a House of God.

Wherever Jews go, they build a House of God. Some temples and synagogues are very, very old; others are very new. Some are built of wood, others of brick or stone. But old or new, brick, stone, or wood, a synagogue is a place where Jews go:

> to pray to God,
> to learn about their religion,
> to meet other Jews.

In this book, we are going to visit a House of God. We will go inside and look at everything very closely. We will find out how Jews pray to God, how they learn about their religion, and how they work with each other. Walk on tiptoe, and speak very softly as we open the big doors . . .

Two
Inside God's House

Feel the quiet!

Feel how God's House is filled with joy, love, and peace!

People have come here to welcome the Sabbath.

The Sabbath is a holy day of peace and gladness.

The Sabbath service is about to begin. The service is the way Jews pray to God together—with prayers and songs and blessings.

The rabbi enters. Often a cantor or other men and women help lead the service. The cantor and the choir sing the songs of the service. All the people join them and give thanks to God. Some of the prayers, like the songs, are in Hebrew. Others are in English. Sometimes an organ plays.

The rabbi lifts a big silver cup filled with wine. He says the **Kiddush.** It is a special blessing for the Sabbath day. The rabbi talks to the people and teaches them about their religion.

Everyone stands and looks toward the holy Ark. The Ark is at the very center of the wall, facing the people. Inside the holy Ark is something all Jews think is the most precious thing in the world: the Torah.

Let us go up and take a close look at the Ark.

Three

We Look Closely at the Holy Ark

In the synagogue is the holy Ark, the **Aron Ha-Kodesh.**

The Ark is where Jews keep the holy Torah.

The Torah tells us how—a very long time ago—God gave Moses the Ten Commandments. These are God's ten most important laws. The Torah also tells the rules for building an Ark, or a box, to hold these laws. The box was to be covered with gold inside and out.

In the days of Moses, the Jewish people lived in the desert. They moved from place to place. So they put poles on the bottom of their Ark. And they carried it wherever they went. When they stopped, they put up a special tent for the Ark. The tent for the Ark and the place around it were called the Tabernacle.

Today, the Ark is not moved. It is no longer like a box. It is more like a closet or cupboard.

Holy Arks are very beautiful. They may have doors of wood, marble, or gold. They may have curtains. The shelves and walls inside the Ark are covered with fine satin or velvet or rich wood.

Four

The Parochet, the Curtain of the Holy Ark

The curtains for the holy Ark in the House of God are very beautiful.

They are made of rich velvet or satin or silk. They are sewed with the finest thread—silver or gold.

Long ago Moses put a curtain in the Tabernacle in front of the holy Ark. He called it a **parochet.** Ever since, the curtain in front of the holy Ark is called a parochet.

Many—but not all—synagogues today have a parochet. It hangs on a rod, so it may open easily.

Sometimes a parochet is very long, hanging from the ceiling to the floor. Sometimes it is short. But it is always beautiful.

The parochet may be changed for different holy days. Special colors—blue or green or yellow—may be used. On the High Holy Days it is pure white.

The parochet almost always has a design on it. Sometimes it has pictures of a lion, a deer, a tree. Often a wide border of gold thread is woven on it. Sometimes it has a Hebrew saying, or the name of the person who gave it.

Five
What Is the Torah?

The Torah is a big book—but it is not like any book you ever saw. It has no pages. It is written on a long, long roll. That is why it is called a **scroll.**

The Torah is not just one book. It is five books. That is why it is so big.

The Torah is all about God. It tells how God made the world and everything in it. It tells how God wants us to live. It tells what God wants us to do. God's laws are in the Torah.

The Torah tells how the Jewish people began. It tells how Moses led the Jews out of Egypt and taught them God's laws. That is why the Torah is also called the Five Books of Moses.

The Torah is so big that it is divided into fifty-four parts. Each part is called a **sidrah.** One sidrah is read every Sabbath morning in the synagogue. The Torah is read through year after year. On Simchat Torah we come to the last sidrah—and guess what happens? We roll the Torah scroll back to the beginning, and start reading all over again!

Six

We Look Closely at a Torah Scroll

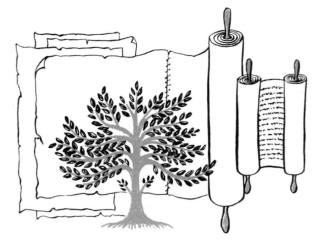

All synagogues have Torah scrolls. Every Torah scroll has exactly the same words. Every Torah scroll is written in the same language—Hebrew.

Torah scrolls used to be written on thick leather. Today, we use the fine skin of sheep or goats. It is washed in a special way and dried. Then it is called **parchment.** Parchment lasts a long time.

A Torah is too long to fit on one piece of parchment. Many pieces are used. They are sewed together to make a long scroll.

Each end of the scroll is then tied to a wooden roller. We call these rollers **Etz Chayim,** the Tree of Life.

Sometimes we call the Torah Etz Chayim, too. This is because Jews think of the Torah as a strong tree. A tree gives us fruit, shade, and wood. We need trees to live. And we Jews need our Torah to live.

Some Torahs are big, others are small. If all Torahs have exactly the same words—how can this be?

The words are always the same, but sometimes they are written in bigger letters.

נש וכה הכה. ידו נרב

כי כספו הוא

או ילדיה. ולא יהיה. אסון ענוש יע

שה. ונתן בפללים. ואם אסון

ת עין שן תחת שן יד תחת רג

ויה. פצע תחת פצע. חת לחבורה. חבורה.

וכי יכה. איש את עין עבדו או את עין אמ

שלחנו תחת ואם שן עבדו או אבר

שלחנו תחת

שור את איש או

אכל את בשרו ובעל השור נקי.

והועד בבעליו ולא. ישמרנו ולא

אם כפר יושת עליו

אב בעליו יומת.

ה חשת עליו. או בן יגח או בת

אם עבד יגח השור או אמ

ודשור יסקל

כהו ויתל ש

Seven

The Sofer
Writes a Scroll

In Bible times, the Torah was not always written down. The wise men learned its words by heart. They taught them to their sons. And the sons taught **their** sons.

Today, the Torah is always written down. The man who writes it is called a **sofer**—he must not make up words. Nor must he leave out words. That is why he says each word aloud before writing it.

The rabbis made many rules for copying the Torah. About 800 years ago, a great rabbi, Moses Maimonides, put all the rules together in one book. Every sofer must follow these same rules.

A sofer must use a special ink, made from the juices of berries and vegetables.

A sofer must use a special long pen, made from the feather of a turkey or goose.

A sofer may not cross out anything. If he misspells the name of God, he cannot even erase it, but he must begin all over again on a new piece of parchment. Sometimes it takes a sofer a whole year to finish one Torah scroll.

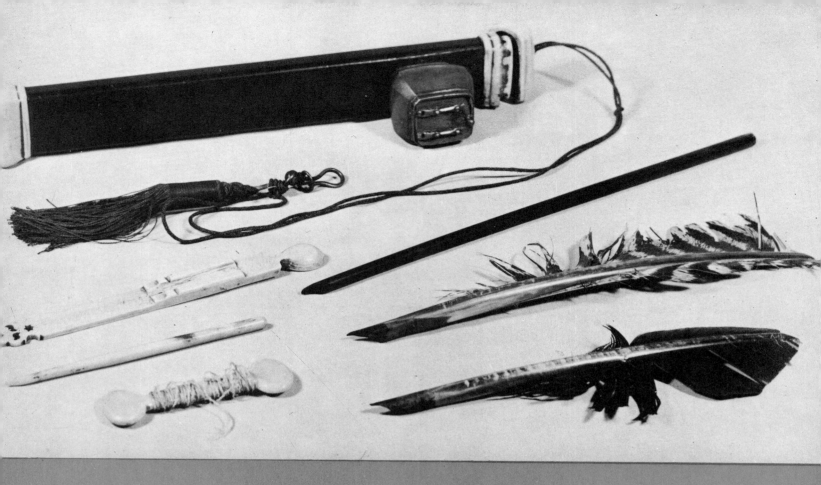

Eight
The Mantle of the Torah

Many Torah scrolls have a special fitted cover made of fine velvet or satin. The covers are called **Torah mantles**.

The mantle is made of rich colors—red, purple, blue, or gold. For the High Holy Days, the Torah scrolls wear mantles of white. This stands for purity or goodness.

After the Torah scroll is read, it is rolled up. A piece of silk or linen holds the two rollers together. The mantle fits right over the top of the Torah. It has two round holes at the top for the rollers to come through.

Jews have always loved to sew pictures and designs on Torah mantles. A favorite picture is a lion, or perhaps, two lions. The lion stands for the tribe of Judah, the tribe of the kings. The Torah is as important as a king—so it, too, has lions.

Sometimes you will see a picture of a deer; or flowers; or the two tablets of the Ten Commandments; or the Sabbath candles. Sayings from the Torah are sometimes sewn on, with gold or silver thread. On some Torah mantles are the names of the people who gave them to the temple.

What picture or design would you sew on a Torah mantle?

Nine

Torah Decorations— the Yad and the Breastplate

A silver chain hangs around the Torah rollers like a long necklace. The chain holds a long rod of silver or gold or ivory. Look at the very end of the rod. See, it is shaped like a tiny hand, with a finger pointing. The word for "hand" in Hebrew is **yad,** so we call this rod a yad.

How is a yad used?

It is used as a pointer! The reader may not use his finger to keep his place in the Torah scroll. So he uses the tiny finger of the yad to point to each letter.

On another chain around the rollers you may see a big, flat piece of silver. This is a **breastplate—**a **tzitz.** Long ago, when the Jews had the great Temple in Jerusalem, the High Priest wore a breastplate like this across his chest. Today, only the Torah scroll wears a breastplate. Often it has tiny bells hanging from it.

Some breastplates have a holder for a special sign. When a temple has many Torah scrolls, one may be set aside for a special holiday. Then its breastplate will say for which holiday it is to be used.

In Honor of
Our Son
D. GOTTLIEB
Nov. 1901

Ten

Rimmonim, Bells, and Keter

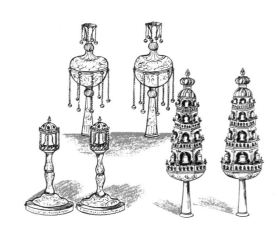

Do you hear the sound of bells?

It comes from two tall silver headpieces. We call them **rimmonim.** They fit over each of the two Torah rollers. Inside and outside the rimmonim hang little silver bells. When the Torah is lifted, the bells ring softly. The bells say to the people, "It is time to hear the words of the Torah." They say, "Stand up! Stand up to honor the Torah."

The Torah is the king of all Jewish books. So, like a king, it may sometimes wear a crown. The word in Hebrew for crown is **keter.** We call this silver crown on the Torah by the same name: keter.

The rimmonim come in pairs. There is one to fit over each Torah roller. But a Torah has only one keter. It fits over both rollers at one time.

Jews believe that a man who is wise in the Torah will be a good man, and try to live a good life. The Torah waits to give its crown to everyone who wants to study.

Eleven
The Menorah

The beautiful, tall candle-holders are the **Menorahs.** Often there are two, one on each side of the Ark.

All Menorahs are not alike. Just as we have many kinds of lamps in our homes, so we have many kinds of Menorahs. Some Menorahs hold little cups of oil. Other Menorahs hold candles. And still others hold electric light bulbs. But all have arms or branches to hold up their many lights.

Count the branches on the Menorah. Does it have seven branches? Most Menorahs in synagogues today have seven branches, but some may have only six.

Why **seven?** Perhaps because there is a branch for each day of the week. Or perhaps because the gold Menorahs in the great Temple in Jerusalem long ago had seven branches. These Menorahs burned olive oil. Every morning priests came to fill the oil cups.

Do you know a Menorah that has **eight** branches? It is the Chanukah Menorah. It has eight—plus one for the **shamash** candle—because the holiday is celebrated for eight days.

Menorahs may be high or low. They may have many shapes. They can be made of gold, or silver, or copper, or bronze, or brass, or even wood.

כי עמד מקור חיים באורך נראה אור

For Thou art the Fountain of life; in Thy light do we see light.

Twelve

The Ner Tamid— the Eternal Light

One light in a synagogue never goes out. It burns day and night. It is always there, glowing softly. It is never turned off. It is called a **Ner Tamid**—an eternal, everlasting light.

Every synagogue everywhere has a light like this hanging over the holy Ark.

Moses put up a Ner Tamid in his Tabernacle. Ever since, a Ner Tamid has burned in the synagogue.

The little Ner Tamid lamps are of many shapes and sizes. They are made of many different metals—gold, silver, brass, or copper. Some have jewels that pick up the light. Others are cut out to let the light come through. Some may use a gas flame. Some may use an electric bulb; some a candle; some oil.

The light of the Ner Tamid shines on the Hebrew words above the holy Ark. The words may say: "Know before whom you stand." Or, "I have set the Lord always before me." The Ner Tamid says, "God is always here."

What do you think of when you see the Ner Tamid?

Thirteen

The Tablets of the Law— the Ten Commandments

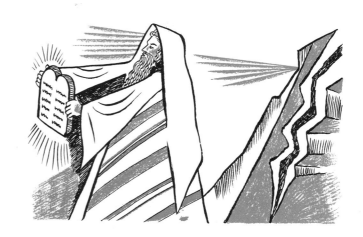

God gave the Jews many laws.

Of all His laws, ten are the most important, the **Ten Commandments.**

Moses wrote the Ten Commandments on stone tablets. He put them in the holy Ark in the Tabernacle. They were called the **Tablets of the Law.**

Many years later, the tablets were lost. But the people remembered the Ten Commandments. They put them in the Torah. When the Torah was written, the people could read all of God's laws—especially the Ten Commandments.

Today Jews still live by these commandments. To help us remember them, some temples have Arks with doors shaped like the stone tablets of Moses. Some have carved the tablets and put them on the wall near the Ark. Very often the words of the Ten Commandments are sewn into the parochet with gold or silver thread.

Because some of the laws of the Ten Commandments are too long to fit on a curtain or an Ark, only the first words or letters of each law may be there, or a number, or a letter.

Fourteen

Art in the Synagogue— Early Times

When Moses built his tabernacle, he called in two skilful artists. "Make the Tabernacle beautiful," he told Bezalel and Oholiab. Both men knew how to work with silver, gold, wood, and stone. They could weave fine cloth of brilliant colors. They built a beautiful Tabernacle.

Ever since, Jews have tried to make their temples beautiful.

How do we know?

We know about early synagogues because we keep finding the ruins of very old ones.

At a place called Dura-Europos, men once dug up a synagogue built 1700 years ago. The walls are covered with wonderful paintings telling stories from the Bible.

Other men, digging at Bet Alpha in the land of Israel, found a synagogue built 1400 years ago. The floor was made of thousands of bits of colored stones, fitted together and called "mosaics." The mosaics are like painted pictures.

Dura-Europos

Bet Alpha

Fifteen

Art in the Synagogue— Today

Today we use fine glass, marble, and rare polished wood and stone to build our temples and synagogues. We plant gardens and trees outside the temple, and sometimes even inside.

Sometimes great artists make stained glass windows with wonderful colors. The sunlight comes streaming through and the whole House of God is full of light.

Painters and sculptors make murals on the walls. Sometimes they are painted on the walls; at other times, the sculptors carve them into wood or stone. Some of the favorite designs are the **Burning Bush,** or a **Menorah,** or a **Ner Tamid,** or a **Magen David.** Many times you will see a **Shofar,** the curved horn of a ram, which is blown on the High Holy Days.

Brass, copper, silver, and gold are sometimes twisted to make special decorations. Often, if you look closely, you see that the shapes are really Hebrew letters. They stand for important words or sayings.

NOT BY MIGHT
NOR BY POWER
BUT BY MY SPIRIT SAITH THE
LORD OF HOSTS

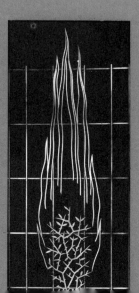

Sixteen
Praying from a Book

When we pray by ourselves, we can make up our own prayers. But in the synagogue, when many Jews come together to pray, all say the same prayers at the same time. They are read from a prayer book, a **siddur.** It means "order," the order of the prayers.

Long ago, Jews did not use books to pray from. The people learned the important prayers by heart.

About a thousand years ago, a great rabbi named Amram gathered all the prayers together and wrote them down in one book.

Later, when people learned to print books, many, many prayer books were printed.

The prayers in the prayer book were not all written by one man. Some come from the Bible. Some were written by rabbis. Others are very beautiful poems. Even when the prayers were put in a book, new prayers kept coming in. Over the years, the prayer book has kept growing and changing.

In every Jewish prayer book, you will find many important prayers written in Hebrew. For many Jews, Hebrew is the most important language of prayer.

Do you know any prayers from the prayer book?

הַיָּמִים · כָּל יְמֵי חַיֶּיךָ
הַלֵּילוֹת · וַחֲכָמִים אוֹמְרִ
יְמֵי חַיֶּיךָ הָעוֹלָם הַזֶּה
כָּל יְמֵי חַיֶּיךָ לְהָבִיא
לִימוֹת הַמָּשִׁיחַ :

בָּרוּךְ הַמָּקוֹם

בָּרוּךְ הוּא · בָּרוּךְ שֶׁנָּתַן תּוֹרָה לְעַמּוֹ
יִשְׂרָאֵל · בָּרוּךְ הוּא · כְּנֶגֶד אַרְבָּעָה
בָּנִים דִּבְּרָה תוֹרָה · אֶחָד חָכָם ·
וְאֶחָד רָשָׁע · וְאֶחָד תָּם · וְאֶחָד
שֶׁאֵינוֹ יוֹדֵעַ לִשְׁאל ·
חכם

הַכָּם
מַה הוּא אוֹמֵר · מָה
הָעֵדֹת וְהַחֻקִּים וְהַמִּשְׁפָּטִי
אֲשֶׁר צִוָּה יְיָ אֱלֹהֵינוּ אֶתְכֶם · וְאַף אַתָּה א
אֱמוֹר לוֹ כְּהִלְכוֹת הַפֶּסַח · אֵין מַפְטִירִין אַחַר
הַפֶּסַח אֲפִיקוֹמֶן ·

רָשָׁע
מַה הוּא אוֹמֵר מָה הָעֲבוֹדָה
הַזֹּאת לָכֶם · לָכֶם וְלֹא לוֹ ·
וּלְפִי שֶׁהוֹצִיא אֶת עַצְמוֹ מִן הַכְּלָל · כָּפַר
בְּעִיקָר

Seventeen

What's Inside a Siddur?

A prayer is what we say or think when we speak to God. The siddur has many different prayers.

Some prayers praise God for His goodness and kindness and mercy. Do you know one that begins, "Praise ye the Lord, to whom all praise is due"?

Some prayers thank God for all He has given us—the Torah, wine, or bread. They begin: "Blessed art Thou, O Lord our God."

Some prayers beg God to forgive our sins. On the High Holy Days, we say: "We have sinned. . . ."

Some prayers ask God for His help and protection: "Grant us peace, Thy most precious gift."

Some prayers comfort us in times of sorrow. They remind us that God is always near: "The Lord is my Shepherd, I shall not want."

Some prayers tell us what to do or remember: "Thou shalt love the Lord, thy God, with all thy heart, with all thy soul, and with all thy might."

Most prayers of the siddur say "us" and "our," not "me" or "I." That is because all Jews are brothers, and we pray together in the synagogue. But even when we pray alone we should never, never forget to care about **all** our brothers.

Eighteen

The Most Important Prayer—the Shema

A long time ago, people prayed to many gods—to the sun or the moon, to trees or to rocks, or even to statues.

Then the Jewish people found there is only One God —the One, True God.

Moses made up a prayer about this. It is in the Torah. Every Jew knows it. It is a prayer he says all his life.

The prayer is called the **Shema.** It says: "Hear, O Israel: the Lord our God, the Lord is One."

Then we praise God like this: "Praised be His name whose glorious kingdom is forever and ever."

The Shema tells us: "Hear, O Israel"—We say to each other and to all Jews: we are part of you, and you are part of us. We are all children of Israel together.

"The Lord our God"—He is not only our God but the God of all mankind. Our people have worshiped Him for a very long time. So always feel close to Him. We want others to feel close to Him, too.

"The Lord is One"—He is the One God for all men, so all men are brothers.

Shema Yisrael, Adonai Elohenu, Adonai Echad!

בל חקתיו ומצות ... יארך ימיך ושבועת ישראל
... וייטב לך ואשר תרבון ... כאשר דבר יי
... אביר לך ארץ זבת חלב ודבש
ואהבת א... אלהינו יהוה אחד
אלהיך בכל לבבך ובכל נפשך ובכל מאדך ...
... האלה אשר אנכי מצוך היום על לבבך ושננ...
ודברת בם בשבתך בביתך ובלכתך בדרך וב...
... על ידך והיו לטטפת בין ...
... מזזות ביתך ובשעריך ...
... אל הארץ אשר נשבע לאבתיך ...
... להתת לך ערים גדלת וטבת אשר ל...
... כל טוב אשר לא מלאת וברת ...
... כרמים וזיתים אשר לא נטעת ואכלת ...
... פן ... אלהי...

DEUTERONOMY

which I command thee, thou, and thy son, and thy son's son, all the days of thy life; and that thy days may be prolonged. 3Hear therefore, O Israel, and observe to do it; that it may be well with thee, and that ye may increase mightily, as the Lord, the God of thy fathers, hath promised unto thee — a land flowing with milk and honey.

4Hear, O Israel: the Lord our God, the Lord is one. 5And thou shalt love the Lord thy God with all thy heart, and with all thy soul, and with all thy might. 6And these words, which I command thee this day, shall be upon thy heart; 7and thou shalt teach them diligently unto thy children, and shalt talk of them when thou sittest in thy house, and when thou walkest by the way, and when thou liest down, and when thou risest... And thou shalt bind... upon thy h...

...for this great fire will consum... if we hear the voice of the Lord God any more, then we shall di... who is there of all flesh, th... heard the voice of the living G... ing out of the midst of the fir... have, and lived? 24Go th... nd hear all that the Lord o... ay say; and thou shalt spe... all that the Lord our God ma... nto thee; and we will hear i... t.' 25And the Lord heard th... your words, when ye sp... and the Lord said unto m... eard the voice of the wor... ple, which they have spok... they have well said... have spoken. 26Oh... uch a heart as this alwa... and keep all My c... that it might be w... and with their childr... Go say to them: Ret... ere by Me, and I... e all the commandme...

...are round about you; 15f... God, even the Lord thy G... midst of thee; lest the a... Lord thy God be kindled ag... and He destroy thee from o... of the earth. 16Ye shall not try the Lo... God, as ye tried Him in... 17Ye shall diligently keep th... mandments of the Lord you... and His testimonies, and His st... which He hath commanded... 18And thou shalt do that whi... right and good in the sight of... Lord; that it may be well with... and that thou mayest go in and pos... the good land which the Lord sw... unto thy fathers, 19to thrust... thine enemies from... the Lord hath...

Nineteen

Singing Songs to God

Singing is another way of praying to God. Singing lets people tell how they feel about God.

Jews were joyful when they thought about God. They made up many songs of praise. One said, "Who is like You, God?" We still sing this very old song — **Mi Chamochah.**

Our songs to God aren't always happy. Some have sad melodies, like the prayer **Kol Nidre** on Yom Kippur eve. Other songs are proud ones, like the **Adon Olam.** This means, Lord of the universe. One of the best known is **En Kelohenu,** "There is none like our God."

The songs of praise are called **hymns.** They began as poems set to music very long ago. Today, composers often take these beautiful old melodies and weave them into new songs. Of course they also write new music for new songs, too.

The man who leads the singing in the synagogue is the **chazan,** or cantor. He sings alone, or with a choir.

One kind of singing you will hear in a synagogue is different from any other singing. It has music like a song, but it has no clear beginning or end. It goes up and down. It grows louder, then softer, and does this over and over again. This is called **chanting.** The chants are the oldest Jewish music.

Twenty

Playing Songs to God

David was a shepherd boy who made up beautiful songs to God.

David became king over Israel. And his son, Solomon, became king after him. Solomon built a great Temple in Jerusalem, where all the Jews came to pray and worship God. They sang the songs of David. They played the harp—and

the *lute*, the *lyre*, the *cythara*, the *cymbals*, and the *drums*

About 2,000 years ago, the great Temple was destroyed. The Jews were so sad they no longer wanted musical instruments in their services. Since that time, they have sung songs to God—but without any instruments.

About 150 years ago, some Jews felt musical instruments should be brought back into our services. So, in many temples today, you may hear an organ. And for special holidays, you may sometimes even hear the harp, cello, violin, or trumpet.

Every temple has one instrument that doesn't make music—it makes a loud, solemn blast. It is the shofar, the ram's horn.

In ancient times, the shofar was used to call the people together. Today we blow the shofar only on the High Holy Days.

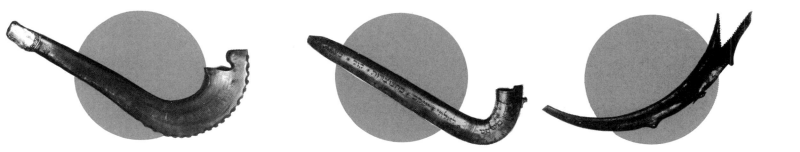

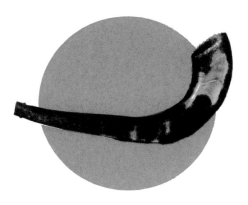

Twenty-One

Why Do We Go to a House of God?

Jews go to the synagogue for many reasons:

> to pray,
> to study,
> to meet.

To pray—at any time. But especially on the Sabbath, and on the holidays, and at very special times, like a wedding or a Confirmation, or a Bar Mitzvah.

To study—all about our religion, our history, our festivals, and our beliefs. We start studying when we are little. We keep on studying for the rest of our lives. Jews want to learn, and this takes a whole lifetime.

To meet—friends, neighbors, and relatives, to pray, learn, and work together. There are meetings and classes. The Brotherhood, the Sisterhood, and the Youth Groups meet in the synagogue to plan ways to help others—the sick, the poor. Children, big and little, come to club meetings and classes—for study, fun, and doing good deeds.

For each person in the family, the temple is a special place of learning, giving, and growing.

Twenty-Two

The Rabbi Is a Teacher

The word **rabbi** is Hebrew for "my teacher."

A rabbi is a teacher. He teaches what it means to be a Jew. He teaches young and old about the Jewish religion and history. He explains God's laws in the Torah. He must go to a special school to learn how to be a rabbi. Afterwards, he must study all his life.

A rabbi is a friend and adviser. The people who come to the synagogue know this. They come to talk to him as a wise friend who can help them.

A rabbi is with us all our lives. We feel close to him at the most important moments of our lives. He offers a prayer when we are born, and when we enter religious school. He teaches us what we must know for Bar Mitzvah and Confirmation. He says the prayers at our weddings, and when life is over.

A rabbi is a leader. He leads the services in the synagogue. He leads the people of his temple in the way they must go to serve God. He works with other leaders in his city to help make life better for everybody.

All through the years the people have turned to their teachers—the rabbis. After the temple was gone, it was the rabbis who taught the people and held them together.

Then as now, it is the rabbi who gives the people courage and faith and hope. He tells them what is expected of them.

Twenty-Three

How Many Rooms in a House of God?

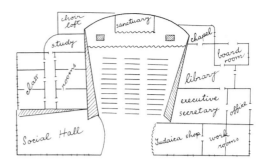

There are many different kinds of rooms in a synagogue.

Do you remember the most important room—the **sanctuary?** That's where the Ark is, and the Torah. It's the room for Sabbath and holiday services. Off to one side may be a smaller room—a **chapel.** People go in the chapel to pray or think alone. Sometimes the daily service is held here.

The rabbi meets people and works in a **study.** If there is more than one rabbi, or if there is a cantor, each one has his study.

The religious school has many **classrooms.**

The people of the temple choose their officers. The officers have a large room, a **board room,** where they hold meetings to make the rules for the temple.

Next to the sanctuary, the largest room of all is the **social hall.** Many people come here for meetings or parties or special celebrations.

A very important room is the **library** for Jewish books. And if you want to buy Jewish books, or other Jewish gifts, you will go to the **Judaica Shop.**

Have we missed any rooms? Yes—the **choir loft** in the sanctuary and the **work rooms** for all the temple workers.

Twenty-Four
Starting a Temple

Many Jewish families have moved to towns—and even countries—where there was no synagogue. How do you think they started a synagogue?

They found other Jewish families living nearby. They met together and decided to form a congregation—one big family—so that all the people could pray together, worship together, and study together.

Where did they meet? Sometimes in a house, or in an empty store, or a hall. Sometimes even in a tent. And the children came to religious school in the store, or hall, or tent.

All the time they were meeting together, they were thinking of ways to build a synagogue and a school. They saved money together, and made plans together.

Months passed, perhaps years. The congregation grew larger and larger. Boys and girls grew up. Little by little, the congregation saved up enough money for a building.

At last their synagogue was finished. The people came together to dedicate it to God. The rabbi said a prayer of thanks. And all the people were proud and happy. They had built a temple for themselves, and their children, and their children's children.

Twenty-Five

How Synagogues Began

The very first Jewish temple was a tent in the desert, called a Tabernacle.

King David decided that Jerusalem would be the chief city for the children of Israel.

King Solomon, David's son, built a great Temple there. The room where the holy Ark was kept was the **Holy of Holies.** It was so holy only the High Priest could enter it—and then only once a year, on Yom Kippur.

The Jews felt that the spirit of God was in the Temple in Jerusalem. They came there to worship, to pray, and offer up sacrifices to God.

But many years later, very wise Jews sensed that God is not just in the Temple of Jerusalem, but that He can be found everywhere, wherever men look for Him. They said: "God is everywhere. You may worship Him everywhere. You can study His Torah everywhere."

So the people began to meet in houses. They called them **synagogues,** after the Greek word for "meeting place."

From that time down to this day, Jews have built synagogues (or temples) wherever they live.

Model of the Temple

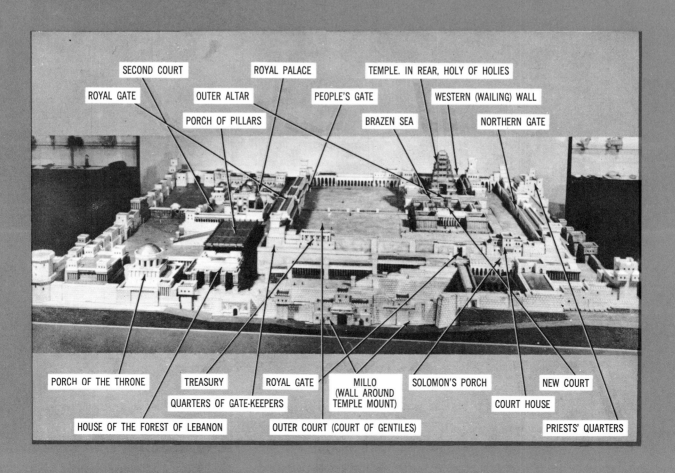

SECOND COURT

ROYAL PALACE

TEMPLE. IN REAR, HOLY OF HOLIES

ROYAL GATE

OUTER ALTAR

PEOPLE'S GATE

WESTERN (WAILING) WALL

PORCH OF PILLARS

BRAZEN SEA

NORTHERN GATE

PORCH OF THE THRONE

TREASURY

ROYAL GATE

MILLO
(WALL AROUND
TEMPLE MOUNT)

SOLOMON'S PORCH

NEW COURT

QUARTERS OF GATE-KEEPERS

COURT HOUSE

HOUSE OF THE FOREST OF LEBANON

OUTER COURT (COURT OF GENTILES)

PRIESTS' QUARTERS

Twenty-Six

The Oldest Temples in the United States

The first Jewish settlers came to the United States in 1654.

They came in a group—twenty-three men and women. They landed in New York. There was no synagogue, for no Jews had ever lived there before. So they held services in their homes.

Later they built a synagogue on Mill Street in New York City. It was the first synagogue in the United States. You can no longer see it—the building is gone now.

As more and more Jews came to the United States, they moved to other places. And they built more and more synagogues. They built them in cities like Savannah, Georgia; Philadelphia, Pennsylvania; Charleston, South Carolina; and Richmond, Virginia.

These early synagogues were very important. They held the Jews together. They also showed Jews in foreign lands that America was free. So more Jews kept coming. The first place they would go was the synagogue. Here they were welcomed and felt they belonged.

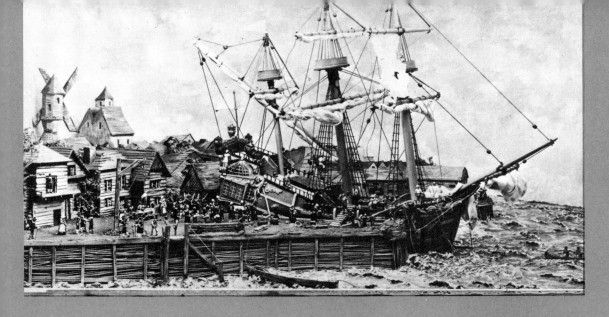

Model of the "St. Charles"; the ship that brought over the first Jewish settlers.

SHEARITH ISRAEL SYNAGOGUE IN THE CITY OF NEW YORK
MILL STREET
1730 - 1817

Charleston, S. C.

Twenty-Seven

The Touro Synagogue

In the city of Newport, Rhode Island, is the oldest synagogue building still standing in the United States.

The synagogue is called the Touro Synagogue, in honor of its first rabbi, Isaac Touro.

The Touro Synagogue opened on December 2, 1763. An English architect named Peter Harrison planned the building. It has 186,715 bricks in it—all brought over from England. No nails were used in building it—only wooden pegs.

Inside at the center is a raised platform, called the **bimah.** The man reading the Torah stood on the bimah. Around the bimah, in a square, are pews. Men sat downstairs. Women sat upstairs in a balcony with a rail around it.

There is a very important letter in the Touro Synagogue. It was written by President George Washington to an officer of the synagogue. It says that all Americans are free to worship God as they wish.

In 1946, the United States government put up a sign saying that the building is a national shrine—important to all Americans.

Twenty-Eight

What Is a Synagogue?

Now you know all about synagogues and temples.

Some may be small, others large. Some may be very simple and plain. Others may have rich designs and rise up toward the sky.

Some may have big round domes. Others may have flat roofs.

Some may be brick or wood; others may be of stone, or marble, or glass.

The outsides may be different. But inside, the things that have meaning to those who come are always the same.

These things are:

a Torah, an Ark,

a Ner Tamid, a Menorah, the Tablets of the Law.

And what else will you remember?

It does not really matter if a synagogue is large or small.

What matters is that the Jews who go there love God with all their hearts. They must try their best

to **learn** God's rules, to **keep** God's rules, to **do** good deeds.

They must learn how to live in peace with each other and with all peoples.

This is what God wants men to do.

And this is what we learn in a House of God.

HEBREW WORDS

Hebrew Word	English Pronunciation and Meaning	Chapter
אֲדוֹן עוֹלָם	**ADON OLAM.** An old song sung in the synagogue. The words mean "Lord of the Universe."	19
אֲרוֹן הַקֹּדֶשׁ	**ARON HA-KODESH.** The place in the temple where Jews keep the Holy Torah. The words mean "the holy Ark."	3
בִּימָה	**BIMAH.** The raised platform in a synagogue where Jews stand to read the Torah. In some old synagogues, the **bimah** is in the very center. In others, the **bimah** is in the front, like a stage.	27
חַזָּן	**CHAZAN.** The cantor.	19
אֵין כֵּאלֹהֵינוּ	**EN KELOHENU.** An old song sung in the synagogue. The words mean "there is none like our God."	19
עֵץ חַיִּים	**ETZ CHAYIM.** The wooden rollers of the Torah scroll. The words mean "Tree of Life." Sometimes we call the Torah itself **"Etz Chayim."**	6
כֶּתֶר	**KETER.** A crown. A king wears a **keter,** and so does the Torah.	10
קִדּוּשׁ	**KIDDUSH.** The special blessing over the wine on Shabbat and holidays.	2
כָּל נִדְרֵי	**KOL NIDRE.** The prayer sung in the synagogue on Yom Kippur eve. The words mean "all promises."	19
מְנוֹרָה	**MENORAH.** The lamp in the synagogue for holding candles, or light bulbs, or little oil cups. Most have six or seven branches, but the **menorah** for Chanukah has eight branches, plus a place for the shamos candle.	11
מִי כָמֹכָה	**MI CHAMOCHAH.** A song of praise to God which comes from the Bible. The words mean "who is like You, God?"	19
מָגֵן דָּוִד	**MAGEN DAVID.** A star with six points. The words mean "Shield of David."	15